You Are VICTORIOUS

SAFIYA AMIRA TERRELL

You Are Victorious

By: Safiya Amira Terrell

ISBN: 978-1987485585

DEDICATION

To my dearest Husband Dexter Terrell: What the enemy meant for evil, God used for our good!

To my one and only daughter Zoen: What an incredible journey that God has taken us both on. Two books in one year! (Mine and yours) May you always know that with the Spirit of God living inside of you, you can do ANYTHING but fail!

To my parents Renard and Sylvia: I love you more than words can describe. Thank you for always being there for me. May you enjoy the fruit of your labor!

To my Aunt Jackie: Truly you are the definition of VICTORIOUS!

To everyone who has poured into me, prayed for me, and impacted my life in anyway big or small I THANK YOU. There are too many of you to name but know that your impression is still upon my heart!

Last but not least to Greg Eldridge: Thank you for your vision and for designing by book cover just as I saw it in the spirit! You are incredibly gifted in more ways than one, and I am excited to see what God is going to do in and through you creatively! You've got next!

INTRODUCTION

Have you ever been at a point in your life where you felt like giving up? Did you ever wake up one day and ask yourself "how did I get here?" Were you ever frustrated about the cards that life has dealt you and no matter what you seem to do, it's a never ending pit that you find yourself in? Are you simply tired of where you are but don't know what to do to get out of your current situation? Do you feel anxiety, worry, anger, sadness, or depression even after you've left the happiest of occasions?

Do you find it hard to trust God? Does it seem like even after all of the years that you have spent learning about God that you still don't seem to have a connection to him? Did you ever feel like after all of your going to church, all of your serving and all of your giving that there still had to be more to God than what you were experiencing? Does it feel like no matter what you do, how much you have or where you go there still seems to be something missing?

If you have answered yes to any of these questions then this book is just for you!

It is with great honor that I assist you, through this book. In **You are Victorious** you will be given the insight, strategies, and arsenal that is needed to take your current situation and turn it around in victory! The skills that you will learn in this book will change your perspective about what it means to have peace, joy, love, and prosperity even in the midst of difficulty. You will learn how to offensively take inventory of your thoughts, feelings, and emotions and not become a victim of Satan's devices. You will learn the dynamics necessary to trust God and grow closer to him in a richer and more meaningful way. Read this book and learn what it takes to become who you already are! For **YOU ARE VICTORIOUS!**

TABLE OF CONTENTS

RUN ON AND SEE WHAT THE END IS GOING TO BE

Spiritual warfare is no joke. We often think of spiritual warfare as a battle we fight whenever the enemy rises up against us but I have learned how inaccurate that thinking really is. Thinking this way is actually what causes us as God's people to fight from a place of defeat or feel like we are always being defeated. It seems like every time we take one step forward in God or even in life, we end up taking three steps backward. It feels like we will never truly get to where God wants us to go or as far as we would like to be in life, when the reality is, we have been looking at this thing all wrong from the very beginning.

For starters, we must realize that we don't prepare ourselves to fight for battle after we have already been hit by the enemy. Rather, we gird ourselves up before it even happens. Some may say "well, why is this even necessary?" Well let me tell you why. Because **fighting the enemy** happens **daily**. We are fighting him when we realize it and even when we don't. The problem is that he is so cunning and deceitful that he will make us **think** that we are not fighting him because of the way he speaks to our minds and hearts. Most of the time **we think that we are actually in the will of God** when in all actuality we are **carrying out the works of our flesh**. Hmmm... something to think about right?

Well let me take it one step further. Remember when Adam and Eve were in the Garden of Eden and they ate the forbidden fruit? (The Holy Spirit has given me so much revelation about their experience that you may find throughout this book that I come back to it over and over again.) Anyway, what I have come to understand is that it wasn't that Adam and Eve thought that they were doing something wrong. In fact they thought in their own minds and hearts that it was God who was keeping them from what they believed would make them have more insight than what they actually had. Sounds familiar?

You see the enemy didn't tell them that he was **warring against them**. He **tricked** them **subtly** and with **cunning deceit**. It was just a normal day in the garden and Adam and Eve had all that they could ever want, think, or imagine. They weren't sick in their bodies. No headaches, no stomach aches, no needing to lay down because they had been tired from working all day. They weren't experiencing exhaustion or dealing with stressors from the cares of the world. No, they were living a day filled with perfect peace and harmony. Which is exactly the point that I am making. They were comfortable, relaxed, and blessed.

So many times we are having these exact same experiences where we are living the good life. We have careers and jobs that give us nice salaries and benefits. We have beaten those health scares and challenges and are physically fit. We have a cozy home to go make our beds in. Our kids are getting good grades in school. We have a spouse or significant other that loves us and will

do anything for us, and we have a great relationship

with our parents, siblings, or friends. Need I say more?

You know, we are for the most part in a good place and

yet even with all that, the enemy gets into our heads

and our hearts to **make us believe that we still need**

more. We **become so comfortable** with life in the

natural that **we forget that we are to be spiritual**. There

is a very profound reason for this and here's why.

Because God's wisdom can only be revealed by the

Spirit. Consider this:

> The Spirit searches all things, even the deep
> things of God. For who knows a person's thoughts
> except their own spirit within them? In the same
> way no one knows the thoughts of God except
> the Spirit of God. What we have received is not
> the spirit of the world, but the Spirit who is from
> God, so that we may understand what God has

freely given us. This is what we speak, not in words taught us by human wisdom but in words taught by the Spirit, explaining spiritual realities with Spirit taught words. The person without the Spirit does not accept the things that come from the Spirit of God but considers them foolishness and cannot understand them because they are discerned only through the Spirit. The person with the Spirit makes judgments about all things, but such a person is not subject to merely human judgements (1 Corinthians 2: 10-15).

What this is saying is that the **world's wisdom and standards are very much different** from God's. It doesn't matter what you have or how much you have, **if you don't have the Spirit of God leading and directing you and helping you to make decisions concerning every area of your life,** then you are just a **sitting duck,** an **open target** that is **waiting for the enemy to walk you** right off a cliff. You **don't have the ability to tap into the supernatural and experience the mind** of God. You won't be able to judge whether or not the next opportunity, no matter how much it glitters, is designed to put you in mental and or emotional debt.

Without the Spirit of God your capacity is limited to understand what is happening in the spiritual realm yet alone how to handle what is about to come down the pike. Because often times, it's how we handle what's coming that determines our next level, and I am not talking about a lateral move, rather a horizontal one upward. One that can only come through the power of God's knowledge, understanding, and wisdom, which is also his Spirit. It's when we walk according to the Spirit that we can see the enemy from far off and not be a victim to his schemes.

So how do we become led by the Spirit? By having the mind of Christ; and how do we obtain the mind of Christ? By daily walking with him, talking to him, and allowing him to be the captain of our ship. We are not in control. We willfully turn our control over to him, and in doing so, **we become** more **empowered to do his will, think his thoughts, go his way, and produce his results**. You see even in Jesus's humanity, he never made a single mistake. He was always in the perfect will of God.

In fact, throughout his journey he actually encountered many demons along life's highway and guess what? He **defeated them all**. Did you hear me? I said, **he defeated them all.** He wasn't duped. He wasn't

tricked. He saw what he saw and called it by name.

Even when Jesus went into the wilderness for forty days

and forty nights and was tempted by the devil, he was

still being led by the Spirit of God. How so? It's quite

simple, he was always connected to the will of his

father. This is why it is so important for us to not get

comfortable in our own beds because we never know

when we are going to **have to stand in the authority of**

who we are in Christ Jesus. Remember, power cannot

be executed in weakness and malnourishment. I mean

think about it. How can a person run with vision if they

are too tired to see?

The Bible is clear that we wrestle not against flesh

and blood (which, in layman's terms, is what we can

see, our situations, our material things, how comfortable we are or not, etc.) but that we wrestle against principalities, wickedness in high places, (which are entities and devices in the spiritual realm) casting down every imagination that exalts itself against God (Ephesians 6:12). If that is the case, which it is, then that means that we must **always be on defense so that we won't be deceived**; and we now know that the only way to do this is **through a deep and intimate relationship with God**, one that is **Spirit led and Spirit filled**. Therefore, we must make a **conscious decision** to **walk** in the **wisdom, discernment, and knowledge** of our **Lord and Savior Jesus Christ,** who never lost at anything.

Now, I will admit that there were definitely other factors to consider for why Adam and Eve ate that fruit, but for the purposes of what I want you to know, right

in this very moment, it is to understand that it was their

comfortability in their circumstance and **their belief in**

their own minds and thoughts that allowed them to be

deceived. So what happens when we are in the place

where we have lost sight and we have begun to look at

our circumstances instead of looking at GOD? What

happens when we have gotten bitten by the venomous

snake and not even realized it because we have allowed

ourselves to be deceived in our own minds and hearts?

What happens when we have believed that we know

what's best for us; and we have begun to move in our

own strength, analyze and evaluate our own situation,

and then take action using our **own wisdo**m? What

happens when we just get too darn comfortable in our

own flesh? Well I will tell you what happens. We end up flat on our faces or on our knees.

There are also other times when the enemy knocks us clean off of our feet, with a hit so hard we feel like we have lost everything. Notice I said **feel** like. Because the Bible declares that our Abba father will **never** leave us or forsake us (Hebrews 13:5) and since he is the mighty King, who created all of the heavens and everything in the earth, whatever you think you lost, or did lose, can be r**estored**. For He is the God of your provision! Now that is what I call unconditional love, grace, and mercy!

However, does being too comfortable come with a cost? Yes. And while that means the road may be difficult, and that you may have to face the music of your actions, know that God is **still** merciful. The Bible says he is **close to the brokenhearted** (Psalm 34:18) and just like he delivered the Israelites out of Egypt, where they lived in trouble and bondage, so too will **he deliver you**. He will restore all of the years that the locust has eaten, the cankerworm, and the caterpillar (Joel 2:25). The Lord will bless you again. He will give you peace again. He will give you joy again. He will give you a new job again. He will give you a new place to live again. He will send you true love again.

Therefore, my brother and my sister, do not get comfortable in your situation. Pick up your bed and walk! Whatever happened to cause you to fall, **get up and keep on moving forward**. Learn the lesson and **gravitate to the grace of God that is available to you.**

Begin to stand up as a conqueror and tell the enemy that you **will not be defeated. Take back** your ownership! Don't look at what is happening around you or even what may have happened to you. **But you must run on to see what the end is going to be!**

Whatever it is that you are going through know that the **fight is already won**! Remember Jesus **defeated every enemy at the cross! You win!** Period! Please don't grow weary while you are going through it because in due season you shall reap a harvest again if you keep on sowing, keep on trusting, and keep on believing GOD. So put on your track sneakers, and **get back in the game!** You can do this! I speak blessings over your life right now in the name of the Lord Jesus. You are the head and not the tail. You are above and not beneath.

You are blessed in the city and blessed in the field. You are more than a conqueror in Christ Jesus! So get up from here so you can **get to your place called next.**

PUT YOUR TRUST IN GOD

I remember my husband and I were having a conversation one night and he told me that during his personal prayer time with God, he asked him how this faith thing worked. He wanted to know how much he actually had to lose before God would come through like he promised. As I rolled that question over and over in my head that night, I could not let it go. I began to realize that at some point in time in our lives, we are all going to have to endure a faith test. Notice I did not use the phrase faith walk, because depending on where you are in life you may be closer to God as opposed to further away, experiencing a season of blessings and favor, and may feel like your walk with God is well, and going along just fine. So faith test seems more appropriate only to make the point that whether you are in a good place or not, no matter if you are walking closely with God or not, or if you have been walking a long time or not, without a shadow of a doubt you will come to a point in your walk where your faith will be tested. As a matter of fact, you will be tested more than once but no matter how you did on the last test, the one that you are currently taking always feels like the first time. Interesting right?

Well God absolutely is interesting and if I could say just one thing about why it feels that way, it would be to assure you that it is because God is taking us from glory to glory and faith to faith (Romans 1:17). That means that God wants to move in our lives in a special way each time like the very first time and here is why.

Because it is as we go through our trials and testing that

our faith is being deepened and it gives another

opportunity for God to bring **glory to his name**. You see,

this is exactly what my husband was experiencing only

he couldn't see it. While he was looking at things from

a natural perspective, God was doing something in the

supernatural. And guess what else? He was calling my

husband to be a divine partaker in the sovereignty of

his grace through this experience. Otherwise, he would

not have allowed him to go through it in the first place.

Was my husband out of a job? **Yes**. Were we

down to one income in our home? **Yes**. Did we have a

mountain of bills to pay? **Yes**. Did one of our cars end

up getting repossessed? **Yes.** Was there food that still

needed to be put on the table? Absolutely **yes**. Was

there college tuition that still needed to be paid? **Yes, yes, and yes again**. But even in the midst of **all** of that God was saying **so what**! None of that means a hill of beans to the one who knows how to **create** the beans. God was **calling** my husband and me to **walk with him in the Spirit!** He wanted us to **experience** him in the **fullness** of his **provision** even though it **seemed** as if we were living in lack. My GOD! You see God was saying if you **become one** with me, if you **trust** me with **all** of your heart and **all** of your soul and **all** of your strength as in accordance with Deuteronomy 6:4-5, then I will give you the grace to walk through this dark valley with **boldness** and **confidence**. He was saying I will rain down manna to you just like I did the Israelites so that you will know that it was I who provided for you, and you will believe without a shadow of a doubt that I **can do**

anything but fail!

Now can you see why there is no way for you to go through the things that you are facing without having your faith be tested? Because what I have come to understand is that a faith that is tested is a faith that is activated! The activation of faith happens because it is based out of what we cannot see. If we knew the how, the when, and the where that God was going to show up then we wouldn't need faith. We would just be walking around and going on with our lives like business as usual. There would be no reason to mention God at all, and we know that definitely does not bring him any glory!

But the Bible says:

> That we are to greatly rejoice, though now for a
> little while you may have had to suffer grief in all
> kinds of trials. These have come so that the
> proven genuineness of your faith—of greater
> worth than gold, which perishes even though
> refined by fire—may result in praise, glory and
> honor when Jesus Christ is revealed (1 Peter 1:6).

So now that we have established that faith tests are

necessary to prove our genuineness then we can

understand why Adam and Eve fell short and ask God to

give us clarity and wisdom so that we don't continue to

make those same poor choices.

Let us be reminded that when Adam and Eve

were in the garden they were, at one point, glorifying

God. The Bible says that God walked in the cool of the

day with them. He had revealed himself to them

because they were operating in his will. So we know

that God was well pleased. But do you know what happened? They **stopped** trusting God. And we know that **without faith** it is **impossible** to **please** God (Hebrews 11:6). You see Adam and Eve wanted to know all the answers to all things instead of **trusting** in the one who is **creator of everything**. What they had was idolatry in their hearts, and what many of us don't understand is that idolatry is not just reserved for the world, but it also includes the body of Christ which I am beginning to see more and more.

There is a great paradigm struggle of power that wrestles deep within us. The struggle to have all the answers, or the struggle to believe God. So let me ask you. What is it that you are struggling with? What is that one thing in your life that you just can't seem to give over to God? Or maybe you have given it over but you are not experiencing any movement yet. You are no further today getting away from it than when you first told God you were going to let him handle it. Have you grown weary? Impatient? Discouraged? Frustrated? Scared? Or angry? Are you ambiguous in any way? You see, these are exactly the kinds of issues that God wants to work out for you but he just wants you to trust him for it.

He never said that you wouldn't have to go through it, but what he did say was that **all things work together** for the good of those that **love God** and are **called according to his purpose**. (Romans 8:28) So know that all is never lost, and even for those things that may not be recovered, the wisdom of God that is gained is

far greater than any tangible object that can ever be received. Sometimes having God's wisdom is the only thing that you need to take along the journey with you so that you can apply this understanding to your next situation or circumstance and have the peace of God that sustains you beyond your wildest imagination!

So today I **prophesy** to you that the **storms of life shall not overtake you**, but that the **Lord's grace shall sustain you**. Now begin to say this prayer out loud so that every negative thought, and every wayward emotion can be destroyed. "Father God, in the name of Jesus, I thank you that your goodness and your mercy is following me all the days of my life as according to your word in Psalm 23:6 and I thank you that you are my strength. You are my rock and you are my deliverer even as you have declared it in your word in Psalm 18:1-2."

"So Lord, I thank you for the activation of my faith today. I will glorify you and sing praises unto your name because you are making my crooked paths straight and you are causing everything to work out for every area of my life. I receive the sovereignty of your grace today and I declare and decree that today I trust you and I surrender everything over to you. Those things that I understand and even that which I do not. I refuse to look at my situation with a natural eye. I will align with your Word and your Spirit because you are the God who knows my end from my beginning. You are the God that has great things in store for me. So I receive it now by faith in the name of Jesus! Amen."

DRINK YOUR WATER FROM THE LIVING WELL

Sometimes the battles we fight are within ourselves. We have sleepless nights, we are full of anxiety and worry, we are looking for love in all of the wrong places, or we have love, and are too demanding. We are trying to live vicariously through our kids, or out-perform someone at work because we are always in pursuit of the next big position. Sometimes we covet after what other people have so we become angry and bitter and begin to spend our money wastefully due to the fact that we are trying to stay current and relevant. Back in the day they used to call it trying to keep up with the Joneses, but whatever you want to name it, it's not being authentic!

We begin living from a place of hurt because we are never satisfied, and out of that hurt, we do whatever it takes to mask the pain. It just ends up being a vicious cycle, a train wreck, a mountain that goes round and round and round. We just keep on pretending, keep on buying, keep on pursuing, and keep on controlling, all in the name of trying to fill a void that is deep within us. You see for a lot of us folks we believe that if we just had one more pair of red bottom shoes, one more diamond bracelet, one more pocketbook, one more car, one more lady, one more man, etc., etc., then we will be fulfilled. But oh, how wrong we are.

You see the infinite God knew what he was doing when he made us in his likeness and his image. The

.em is that not many of us truly know what this really entails. Have you ever stopped to think about it? Really...what **does** it mean to be created in his image and likeness? Well let me drop this little nugget into your spirit. What it means is that the essence of your being is **infinite** just like GOD. Still don't understand? Well let me break it down a little further. Being infinite means that there is no beginning and no end, that it goes on and on forever and guess what? That same definition applies to your inner being as well! All of the desires and longings that are within you literally go on and on forever too. It never stops because you were created **for** Him! Now that's what I call an aah-haa moment. Now that you know this to be true it should begin to make sense why there is such a deep craving within you. No matter what you do or how much you try to obtain in life, even if you get that one more house, that ten thousand dollar a year increase in salary, marry the man or woman of your dreams, you will always feel like you want more and more. Your soul will **never** be filled and will **never** stop searching until you find **rest** in Him. He did it that way **purposely**. No matter where you go or what you acquire, the seat of your soul will never be fulfilled until you are **connected** to Lord of all creation.

This is why you can see someone who doesn't have a whole lot but they are just as happy and content as they want to be. They are rich in spirit! They know who they are because they have been plugged in to the creator; the power source! And because they are connected to the infinite one, there is no more need to

seek just one more of anything because He is the one

that has it all. **HE IS THE INFINITE ONE!** Hallelujah; and

because I really need to drive this point home, let's take

a look at a passage of scripture in John 4:4-26.

Here in this story we find that there is a woman

at the well who has an encounter with Jesus. This is a

woman who had slept with various men and came to

the well to get a drink of water. As she was talking with

Jesus he said to her "this water that I have, you will

never thirst again". That statement holds so much

significance, such incredible weight because even

though she kept coming to that well due to the fact

that she was physically thirsty, Jesus was letting this

woman know there was an inner thirst within her that

could never be quenched no matter how many lovers she had. He was telling her that none of those encounters, no matter how good they made her feel, would ever be able to fill her void. But the great news in all of this was that Jesus was giving her notice that she no longer had to look for anything! Her endless search was over, for she had been met with the **infinite** God who could meet all of her **infinite** needs!

Do you see what I mean now? For Jesus said that he is the **living water**. He is the **bread of life** and what I find to be so fascinating is that he chose to compare himself to the things that human beings seem to need the most...**food and water!** You see Jesus was having a human experience and he realized that nutrition is what we identify with as the most necessary and basic need to maintain our bodies and keep us alive and yet

he was using the statement to make the exact opposite

point instead! What Jesus was actually saying was that

while it is a fact that your body needs food and drink

we must also realize that these things will **not** be

enough to **quench** our **deepest** hunger, or our **deepest**

thirst, which can only be **filled through him**. For the

Bible declares that man shall not live on bread alone

but by every word that proceeds out of the mouth of

God (Matthew 4:4).

Therefore we can easily see all the more how

Adam and Eve messed up big time. They were living life

on top of the world. I mean they had dominion over

everything. Can you imagine having everything at your

very fingertips? Can you just envision everything that

you've ever wanted belonging to you? Financial security done. Children's college tuition done. Vacation trip done. New house done. Designer clothes done. Now, in no way, am I placing emphasis on material things over GOD but that is just my point. That because they were **in** GOD and **connected to him**, he **gave** them provisional blessings! They didn't lack for **anything**. That was the way it was **intended** to be. So I believe it is important that we get a good picture of how much our Daddy in heaven **loves us** and how he wants nothing but the **absolute best for us**. Period.

Adam and Eve never said oh, we are hungry, oh we are thirsty, and oh we are bored, no, never not even once. That is because they were connected to the infinite one, so all of their infinite desires were met. It wasn't until they were deceived into believing that they didn't have everything, that they cut themselves off from their source. That is when they realized they were missing something. No longer were they content. Their eyes were opened to the realization that there was such a thing called **separation**, something GOD **never** wanted them to experience. He knew separate from him, they would always be looking to fill that void.

Adam and Eve turned from the **infinite** one and towards the **finite** one. Remember, Satan is a **created** being, which means his time will come to an end. You see Adam and Eve had put someone else in the place where God was supposed to be. They thought that something created could fill their infinite need. Get it? And where did it lead them? To a life of sin, destruction, and death. Isn't that the same thing that we are facing

today? For the very same reasons?

But thanks be unto GOD that he is our deliver. For

the Bible declares that he will **always** provide a way of

escape. No temptation will we endure that we won't be

able to stand (1 Corinthians 10:13). My brother and my

sister, today make a declaration to get back in right

position with the one true living GOD. Repeat these

words after me. This is your prayer of cleansing. "Father

God in the name of Jesus, forgive me for not being

connected to you. Forgive me for putting people,

things, and accomplishments in your place. For you are

Sovereign. You are the infinite one. I turn back to you

because it is only in you that the essence of my being is

fulfilled. Fill me up with your abundant love and your

everlasting Spirit. Make me whole in you so that I can

live a victorious life. In Jesus name!"

CLOTHE YOURSELF IN RIGHTEOUSNESS

When I think about putting on any type of

clothing, the first question that I ask myself as I look in

the mirror is, "how does this look?" Typically if I like the

way the clothes look on me, then I will feel good when I

wear it. Why? Because what we wear says a lot about

how we feel about ourselves. Let us consider the

following factors so you can better understand what I

am conveying. Disheveled clothes may reveal you are

going through a crisis, while wrinkled clothes may

indicate that you were rushing or don't have the time.

After all, there are just times when we have too many

responsibilities and not enough hours in a day. We've

all been there and had days like this. I know I have.

Sometimes too many to count. A suit and tie could

mean that you are preparing for a business meeting or

you are a leader within an organization or company.

Even uniformed attire like that of a fire fighter or police

officer indicates courage and honor. Do you see where I

am going with this? What we wear is in fact a

representation of who we are.

Now don't get me wrong, in no way am I saying

that our clothes **DEFINE** who we are, but it is a

reflection of us in one way or another. Let's be honest.

Who wouldn't feel good after taking a nice hot shower

or bath, putting on a gown or tux, getting their hair

professionally done or cut, and topping it all off with

the best of perfume or cologne? That's right. I can't

think of one soul whose confidence wouldn't boost even if only for a little while! I am sure that you can't either. Well, since that is the case, don't you think the same thing happens when we clothe ourselves in the righteousness of God?

Before we answer that question I think it's important for us to take a step back and dissect why this righteousness is so significant to begin with. For starters, if someone can be clothed and covered up then that means that they can also be naked and exposed. So let's go back to Adam and Eve again. You see God was very strategic when he created them in nakedness. For one thing God could have given them something to put on their bodies right after creating them but he didn't. Why do you think that was? Well let me tell you. Because God is **ALL WISE.** Nakedness represents vulnerability. Vulnerability also gives way to transparency and truth, and when you are in a relationship with someone, these components are required. Simply put...these were the characteristics that God had placed within Adam and Eve. These qualities were facets of himself that he wanted Adam and Eve to give back to him. After all, that is what a relationship does. It gives and it receives. It's called reciprocity. Let's go deeper.

Clearly, it was always God's desire that human beings live freely in him. For it is in him that we move, live, and have our being (Acts 17:28). Not only did this nakedness signify truth, it also created an intimacy between God, Adam, and Eve that signified their oneness and their union. It was a bond that was never meant to be broken. But much like what happens to any relationship when lies and deceit comes in, trust is broken, hearts are shattered, and healing needs to take place. Sounds familiar? You see, after Adam and Eve were deceived they ran from God and hid themselves. The Bible says they realized they were naked and they were ashamed. Think about it for a minute. Why would they run and hide if they were naked all the time? Because in reality it wasn't their nakedness that they were ashamed of. It was the sin that they committed which made them feel guilty. So they tried really hard to hide it. Isn't that what we do when we are guilty, embarrassed, or ashamed? We run and hide. We don't want to address it or admit it. It has a way of making us feel icky inside, where all we want to do is bury it in the closet in hopes that it never finds us.

Remember, the enemy's number one job is to keep us separated from God. He wants us to take cover and hide ourselves from the only one who truly knows all about us. Now, you tell me, what does this better than sin? Deep down inside we know that we are in need of help and healing but we are either too prideful to admit it or too ashamed of what we have done. You see the enemy **KNOWS** this. He is the father of lies, and these are the things that he repeatedly speaks to our hearts and minds. He tells us that we are unworthy. He strives to make us think that God will never see us the same. He tries to convince us that a particular sin is unforgivable. He attempts to make us believe that we don't deserve healing simply because we were the

victimizer, and when he does this, the vicious cycle

continues. As a result, generation upon generation is

affected by our hidden pain.

So whether you know it or not, that is exactly

what Adam and Eve had... pain that they were trying to

hide. Their lack of ownership of that pain, their need to

blame one another instead of standing in the middle of

it and admitting that they needed help with their sin is

ultimately why God made them clothes and sent them

away from the Garden. Yet, even though God did this,

he knew what they didn't know. God understood that

Adam and Eve traded in their reflection of himself for

clothes of sin. He also knew that there would be

nothing that they could ever put on that would make

them feel as whole and secure as before they ate that fruit. For the rest of their lives they would be supplementing for what only comes from being in union with him.

But this was not just true for Adam and Eve but for **ALL** of humanity. After all, isn't that why we needed a Savior? Doesn't that explain why Jesus hung himself high and stretched himself wide **WILLFULLY** on the cross for us that we might be reconciled back into right standing with the Father? Isn't that why, when his blood was shed for us, it covered a multitude of our sins, all because he loved us (1 Peter 4:8) and wanted us redeemed? For the Bible declares that it is not his will that even one of us shall perish (2 Peter 3:9).

You see it is the blood of Jesus that clothes us in righteousness. His blood takes all of our sins, all of our dirt, and all of our mess and makes us without spot or blemish (Ephesians 5:27). For Jesus was the perfect lamb, free of sin, free of error, free of blame and he traded places with us. He took on every affliction and every burden. He carried the weight of our depression, our lies, our pride, our bitterness, our envy, our anger, our stealing, our rebellion, our fornication, our abortions, our adultery, our homosexuality, our selfishness, and whatever else is imperfect and flawed. He felt our hearts and read our minds and embodied all of who we are even though he didn't deserve to. He did that all for you and all for me simply because he loves us and did not want anything to separate us from that love. Yes you heard me right. Even though we have been getting it wrong since the fall, he paid the ultimate price so that we could be **set free** from it all. Jesus!!!

Now we can answer the original question of why we must clothe ourselves in the righteousness of God. When we immerse ourselves in seeking to understand why Jesus died for us, we realize that life nor death, nor angel, nor demon, nor heaven, or hell can ever separate us from the love of God for those who are in Christ (Romans 8:38). For it is **this knowing** that fortifies us and strengthens us. It is **this understanding in Christ** that gives us this confidence and **qualifies us** to receive this righteousness. Oh, it is ours! The blessings do belong to us! God says that we are heirs to the throne

(Romans 8:17)! There is divine power and access to God's kingdom when we stand in our rightful place! But to be clothed in righteousness means that we must be soaked in his word, and drenched in his presence so that he can reveal the truth of who we are in him. There is without a shadow of a doubt no way that when we do this we won't begin to sing new songs unto him and burst forth with joyful melodies. God will begin to cloak us in his garment of praise, multiplying his grace, joy, and peace, to us because we have become partakers in his divine nature!

So my brothers and my dear sisters, do not let what has happened to you or even what you may be currently going through right now to keep you from the All Knowing one. He knows your end from your beginning, (Isaiah 46:10) and he wants you to be in perfect union with him. Malachi 3:6 says, "For I am the God that changes not." God says this because he wants you to know that he is full of love and mercy. He is always waiting for **you to turn your heart towards him** so that he can turn towards you. No sin is too great. There is no mistake that can't be erased. Clothe yourself in the righteousness of God so that you can receive the great promises that he has in store for you.

So Father God, in the name of your son Jesus, I thank you that the person who is reading this right now knows that you love them, and knows that they are worthy of salvation, wholeness, healing, and blessings. Wash them in your blood right now, Lord and reveal to them the truth of who you are. For there is healing in you. There is deliverance in you, and there is freedom in you. Now say this prayer over yourself. "Heavenly Father, in your Word, Romans 8:1 says that there is no condemnation for those that are in Christ Jesus and because I belong to you the power of your life- giving spirit has freed me from the power of sin that leads to death. Also, according to your word in Ephesians 2:8, I have been saved by grace through faith which you have given to me freely as a gift. Therefore I am worthy, I am called, and I am chosen, and I am loved. I am clothed in your righteousness! I receive it and believe it in Jesus Name!"

ENDURE THE MAKING PROCESS

The making process is not always easy but, my God, it is necessary. Sometimes we can get so busy with our day to day activities, our daily routines, and the demands of our lives that we forget that we belong to GOD. We are often so stretched to the point that we can't even think of doing just one more thing. After all there are only so many hours in a day, right? Wrong. God is the last person (and I don't mean that he is a person literally) for whom this will ever matter because he orchestrated time, and space as well. He is the infinite God, who lives outside of time, so that is not an excuse that He is willing to hear. You see, God knows how much we need him, and he knows those hidden things which shape us even though we can't see them.

The Bible tell us that God knew who we were before he formed us in our mother's womb (Jeremiah 1:5). Even in his love he chose us before the foundations of the world (Ephesians 1:4). Interestingly, we only know ourselves from the perspective that we can see but God sees us from the place of our creation all the way through to our destiny.

This thoroughly explains why we tend to feel so much anxiety and fear over the future. Since the human eye can only see so far, we do not know the end result. No matter how smart we are, how many degrees we may have, how much money we saved in the bank, we cannot predict the future. Now I know you may be thinking to yourself, well, God speaks to me, he shows me things to come and that may be true. Our GOD is

GRACIOUS and it is his desire that we have access into his thoughts, his heart, and his will for our lives but he doesn't tell us all of the details! If he did then he wouldn't be GOD and there would be no need to trust him.

Which brings me to my next point about Adam and Eve. Because they were made in God's likeness and image, just like us, they indeed had access to his thoughts, his heart, his provision, and his will. It wasn't until after they separated themselves from their relationship with him that they lost sight. You know that really does explain why non-believers and even believers for that matter are walking around so blind, and so lost. I have to mention the believer because so many of us are still doing this as well. Despite the fact that we are going to church week after week, and serving on ministry after ministry, we are **still not** in relationship with him. We are walking around **cut off**.

Yet this was not God's intention for Adam and Eve and it is not his intention for any of us either. Jesus said, I come that you might have life and have it more abundantly. (John 10:10) This means when he went to the cross at Calvary, he wasn't **just** dying for our sins, he was also **restoring** what was lost! He died so that we could take our rightful positon in the kingdom. The cross is where we gained our access! It's where we gained the victory! To sit in heavenly places, yes. However, the access is also granted to us right here and right now as well! This access is given to us to **teach** us how to live our best lives on earth in the **fullness** of peace, in the **fullness** of joy, in the **fullness** of our

dreams, in the **fullness** of our creativity, in the **fullness**

of riches, in the **fullness** of prosperity, and in the

fullness of love. Now that is what I call **abundance**!

Sadly enough though, some of us never fully

grasp it and spend so much of our lives struggling to get

out of the pit. We go on believing that it's just part of

our reality to be depressed, confused, heart broken,

and hopeless. Now please, by no means am I excusing

the fact that we have challenges and issues that have

changed the course of our lives. But what I am saying is

that from the first day in the garden, Satan's number

one job has been to cut off our relationship with God so

that we don't know who we are! He hasn't stopped!

He is still on his assignment, therefore, we must be on

ours! Remember, the Bible says that he roams around like a lion to seek whom he may devour (1 Peter 5:8). This means he is plotting on those who are cut off from relationship with GOD. Those who do not know who they are. Those who are not fighting **from** a place of victory.

One of the most incredible examples that I can give would have to be the story of Job. In the Bible, Job is described as a mighty man of God that walked faithfully with Him. But GOD allowed Job to lose it all. He lost his family. He lost his friends. He lost his health. He lost his provision. Everything that you can think of, Job lost it. Yet there was one thing that he didn't lose and that was his intimacy with God. Since he was still able to access the Father through their relationship, that is what made all of the difference. Because Job

knew who he was he remembered the Lord's promises

and guess what? GOD came through! The Bible says

that when the enemy comes in like a rushing flood, the

Spirit of the Lord will **lift up a standard against him**

(Isaiah 59:11). God restored double for Job's trouble.

Literally! Everything that Job lost, God gave it back to

him twice. Jesus!!!! Now that's what I call restoration!

Now why is this so important? Because in all

actuality what Job endured and what he had to go

through was really all about his **identification**! Job

remained so **connected** to the source that God had to

come through for him! The Bible says that the Lord is

watching and he **will certainly carry out all of his plans.**

(Jeremiah 1:12) When you are not persuaded by

outside influences and you stand firm in the Lord, he must **honor** his word. For the Lord our God is faithful to the faithful (Psalm 18:25). If only Adam and Eve had not been so easily persuaded, think of how the Lord would have moved on their behalf. Can you now see the tactic of the enemy? Do you see how he wants for you to **move out** of **position?** In both cases, Adam, Eve, and Job were all going through **spiritual warfare**. This warfare was between the force of light which is God and the force of darkness which is Satan.

While all three of them were tempted, it was Job that passed the test. Adam and Eve allowed the enemy to use them, but Job, who truly demonstrates the greatest example of faith in my opinion, stood on the word of God. Which is exactly the point that I am making. Sometimes we have to do just that. Stand and wait for the Lord to deliver us, because he always saves, he always delivers, and he always sets free. Even when it gets **uncomfortable** and **difficult** we must **not** let the enemy **trick us**. I know I have already said it before but let me say it again. For we fight not against flesh and blood but against principalities and wickedness in high places (Ephesians 6:12)! Satan is not human, he is a spirit being, but guess what? He is **not God** and that's what we have to remember! Just like God created us, he created him too, and when we understand that the battle we are in is not really about us, but rather who we belong to, then we can wait patiently in the fire knowing that we will come out refined. For that is what happens when gold and diamonds are placed in the fire. They are formed. They take shape so that they can be made in to something great.

So it is the same with us. Sometimes we are just going through life and we are not being replenished. Other times we are in desperate need of our source and don't even realize that we are thirsty. Moreover, there are also times when we are running on empty and are oblivious to the destruction that we have allowed ourselves to be deceived by and caught up in. My brother, my sister, when this happens, GOD will make us to lay down in him. He will force us to bow and prostrate before him when all is lost, when we are broken, and when we have been doing things separate from his will. Where all we can do is cry out to the Savior and say, "Help me Lord! Forgive me for my ways!" Because believe it or not, it's the **submission** that takes place before Him that **determines** the **transformative level** of our **making process**. God has all the time in the world and because he is so GOD he will **make us** again and again, allowing us to **go through** many levels of corrections and afflictions until we **willfully** lay it all down at his feet.

The beauty in all of this is that being made to lay down in Him is our place of safety. It is our fortress and it is our sanctuary. It is the only abode where we can be one with the Father and be reminded of who we are and whose we are. For the Bible says, He makes me to lie down in green pastures. He leads be beside the quiet streams (Psalms 23:2). You see God is so good because as he begins to meet those needs and restore your soul, you realize that he is your provision and your source for everything. All of those empty and dead places in your life suddenly become green and alive. God is so good to us when we realize it and when we don't. Full of mercy and unmerited grace. So as you are being made to lay down in his pasture, and take rest in him, know that he is making you into who he wants you to be and don't resist him. Allow him to have his way in your life. You are being made to bring him Glory.

This is what I want you to do right now. Take your hand and place it on your chest, close your eyes and utter these words. "God, thank you so much for loving me. Thank you that you know me better than I know myself. Thank you for making me to lay down in green pastures, and thank you for leading me beside the quiet streams." Now speak to your situation or your circumstance like you know that you already have the victory! Come on, you can do this. Say it from your belly! "Even though I am walking through the darkest valley right now I will fear no evil! For God's rod and staff is comforting me. He is preparing a table for me in the presence of my enemies. He is anointing my head with oil right now and I am dwelling in the house of the Lord even as I speak. I am being made right now. Made to be better, made to be stronger, made to be blessed. In Jesus Name!"

DWELL IN THE SECRET PLACE

One of the hardest things to do in life is not look at the natural circumstances that are staring you smack dead in your face. It's easy to believe God for other people or to have a positive outlook on things when you are not the one being personally affected by the situation. But oh, once those tables turn, that is when what is truly down on the inside of you will manifest itself and show you just where you truly are. It is in the times of our own hardships that we need to hear more than our own voice. Philosopher Daisaku Ikeda once said that a person's true nature is revealed at times of their greatest adversity.

So if that is the case, what do you do when you don't have all of the answers? What is your vice when your back is up against the wall? How do you respond

when you have been betrayed? How do you react when

the doctor's report is filled with uncertainty? Do you

find comfort in the relationship of your parent or a

close relative? Could it possibly be your spouse,

significant other or best friend? Is it an outlet that you

physically partake in? Exercising, drowning yourself in

the t.v., throwing yourself into extra work, clubbing,

drinking, sexing, overeating on food, gambling, or

taking all that frustration out on your children? Is it

listening to your favorite preacher or motivational

speaker that you like to periscope or find on YouTube?

Whatever it is, I can guarantee that if you do it long

enough it will begin to shape your thoughts, your

feelings, your attitude and your behaviors. Simply put

whatever or whichever the thing is that you give your

attention over to the most is what will contribute to the

formation of your character.

So while it is true that we need to hear more than

our own voice, the thing that we give ourselves over to

is what will determine the voice that we hear the

loudest and the clearest. Make no mistake about it, it's

that same voice that you hear the loudest that will be

the voice that drives your next decision and do you

know what I find to be the scariest part of it all? The

justification that comes afterward. Oh yes, the Bible

says that as a man thinks in his heart so is he (Proverbs

23:7) and then it goes to say that there is a way that

seems right in the sight of man (Proverbs 14:12). Now

while these two scriptures are using different

vernacular it is clearly saying the same thing. Once we have decided to feed our spirit anything more than the presence of God then we have just opened the door to enemy's territory and have allowed him free reign to access our hearts, our thoughts, our emotions, and even the will for our lives.

We give him the power to seduce us and set booby traps all around us. We don't even know that we are caught until all of a sudden we find ourselves struggling and what's even sadder than this is we can't even figure out why! All of a sudden we are angry, emotional, frustrated, nasty, blaming everyone under the sun. Yet never once have we stopped to look at the man in the mirror and say maybe it's me. It is my character that is flawed. My perception that is off. My thinking is skewed. My actions are immature. My motives are impure. My energy is negative. You see this is why dwelling in the secret place is not an option but a **necessity**! We need the presence of God to **consume** us and his Spirit to not just dwell dormant in us but **pump** through our very veins, giving us the oxygen that we need to breathe, the clarity that we need to think, the revelation that we need to hear, and the wisdom that that we need to respond.

What I have personally learned about the dwelling of the secret place is that it teaches you how to stand in the midst of the battle. It is the place where the promises of God become magnified! The Bible says that when trouble is all around us, God will rescue us from every trap and protect us from every disease. He will cover us with his feathers and he will shelter us with his wings. The Lord's promises will be like an armor of protection (Psalm 91:3-4). You see, here is the thing about the word of God, it is alive and it is active if you put it in action! Remember that Jesus was literally the word of God made flesh and because he lives then the word lives too! It is not something that we just read. Rather, it is something that we consume, that we become, that we pursue, so that we can bring forth the promises that have already been decreed for us before the foundations of the world.

When we make the word of God and his presence our living quarters then not only are we covered under the shadow of his wings but we do not fall victim to Satan's devices and schemes. The dwelling place actually **fortifies** and **strengthens** us so much to the point that when others are fearing the enemy's super tactics and forgetting his subtle ones we will literally be able to **WALK OVER** them! You will not be railroaded into making unwise decisions. Unlike Adam and Eve, you will not come into agreement with the destruction or annihilation that is set up for your life. The Bible says that no evil will conquer you and no plague will come near your home. You will be able to trample upon lions and cobras and you will be able crush serpents under your feet (Psalm 91:10, 13).

You see we often think of plagues as just a physical sickness that is contagious but did you know that plagues also afflict? That's what a plague is by definition...affliction. One that causes burden and harassment. Plagues are designed to torment, curses and trouble as well. Isn't the correlation between this and Satan's assignment obvious? Remember, his job is to **steal, kill,** and **destroy**. **Plague**! His job is to keep you **distracted** and **disillusioned** into doing your own thing so you and your children can become the next targets. **Plague!** Let me put it to another way, when we are not dwelling in the secret place of God we leave ourselves **exposed**, **uncovered**, and we make room for **infection** to hit, coming right up to our front door, and enter in. The problem with all of this that I am continually seeing more and more is that many of us are walking around with infections that are lying dormant within us. We have no idea that we have been hit until it manifests into a **full blown disease**!

The Bible says do not give the enemy a foothold (Ephesians 4:27). Let us recall that Adam and Eve spent time with the snake. They entertained him and he even convinced them that he was **for** them. Isn't that what the enemy makes us think when we are dwelling in other places and things more than we are dwelling in the secret place of God? He makes it seem so innocent, so socially and culturally acceptable. When Adam and Eve were being befriended by the enemy they had no idea that a plague was coming to their family. They had no idea that their future son, Cain, would murder his brother and their other beloved son, Abel, due to the generation sin that they were responsible for passing down. Even though the secret place was available to them, they did not dwell it in. So right now I ask you these two questions. What is taking up residence in your house? Who is living in your castle? If for any reason the answer is something other than God then what has happened is your relationship has been compromised.

Therefore I want to pray this with you right now. Father God in the name of Jesus help my sister or brother that is reading this to realize that you are the beginning and the end and everything that is in between. Give them the ability to know you as Almighty and to seek you as King. Uproot every distraction, hindrance, disturbance, that seeks to destroy, destruct, and disenfranchise their dwelling place in you. Expose every trap, every trick, and every deceptive motive that is used to disguise the plan of the enemy. Make them rise up and awaken to your purpose and your agenda

that is of substance and abundance. Hide them Father

under the shadow of your wings! While they are resting

and dwelling in you, teach them your word, teach them

to war, and teach them how to win! In Jesus Name!

LET PEACE BE YOUR WEAPON

Many people see peace as being a sign of

weakness, especially if it means turning the other cheek

and walking away in retreat from what you know would

otherwise be a good enough reason to stand and fight.

Today I want to pose to you this question. How can

peace be used as a weapon when it is designed to make

you be still? For starters notice that I said **be** still and

not stand still. That is because in order for anything to

be a weapon it must be designed to cover and protect

you in some way. Sometimes the weapon can be used

to aim, or hit, the oncoming opposition. Other times

weapons can be used to guard your entire body from

head to toe regardless of whether you are sitting,

standing, kneeling, walking, or talking. At times the

weapons are also made to be hand held. So while they may not be able to shield your entire body all at once, the weapon has been designed for you to move into whatever position the body is that has the potential of being harmed. In either case they are all used to be able to guard against whatever is coming toward you that poses potential harm. This in itself is so important to understand because the position that your body is in, regardless to whether you are kneeling, sitting, or standing, is irrelevant. On the contrary what is of importance is the WEAPON being able to **function** properly in whatever current state your body is in and guess what my brothers and sisters, that is exactly what **peace** is **designed** to do!

The Bible says those who keep their mind stayed on me, I will keep them in **perfect peace** (Isaiah 23:3). This means that no matter what is going on around you, in front of you, on the side of you, in back of you, on top of you or beneath you, you won't go crazy, you won't lose your mind, you won't want to take your own life or anybody else's for that matter, because you will be in a state of peace. Peace that surpasses all understanding! You see the enemy wants us to believe that just because we don't know the outcome that we are going to suffer, that just because tragedy struck, we will never smile again. He wants us to feel that just because we made a terrible mistake we are useless. That just because we were embarrassed when we lost our jobs, we can't face tomorrow. But thanks be unto

GOD that when we put our minds in Christ Jesus **all** roads lead to him and after reading a few pages of this book you should know by now that it means we win! That's right we win, again!

So no matter how many times we fall down, no matter how many turns our lives take, no matter how many scary moments present themselves, the Lord Jesus Christ is the victorious King and those who are in him have the victory too! The key though is that you must be **in** him. Jesus himself said to the disciples that he was the **true vine** and that they were **the branches**. That as long as the branches were connected to the vine they would **live,** but those who **were separated would wither up and die** (John 15:5-6). Unfortunately, Jesus was not just talking about a natural death but he was also talking about an emotional and spiritual death as well.

Think about the numerous amount of people that are dealing with depression on a daily basis. Those that can't seem to get a grip on life because they are stuck in the past. How do you suspect they got there? It certainly didn't happen because they wanted it to. Sadly more times than not, people's minds get stuck on the circumstance and they just can't seem to shake it off. Sometimes those stuck feelings lead to unforgiveness, bitterness, and resentment, so life just keeps on giving them the same deck of cards over and over and they can't figure out why.

Do you see how the power of the mind when focused on the same thing over and over can cause you to feel drained, lost, and unhopeful? These are definite signs that someone is withering slowly into death. Yet, before we go any further let's think for a minute who else withered slowly into death because they were not using their weapon of peace? That's right. Adam and Eve.

Now, let's examine the facts. The fact of the matter is Adam and Eve lived in the Garden of Peace. How do I know it was peaceful? Because it was the perfect environment created by a perfect God for human beings to live in. So why is it then that if the garden was peaceful and perfect, once the enemy came upon them with his cunning and manipulative tricks that they fell for his deception? Well it is quite simple. Because their minds were not on **who God said they**

were. Their minds were on **what Satan said they would be able to achieve**. See it doesn't matter whether what has been achieved is a good thing or bad thing. If it isn't lined up to who God says you are, (remember he said that he is the vine and we are the branches) then it's not in connection to him. Also, what else did we say earlier? That if the branch is not connected to the vine that it withers up and dies. Adam and Eve didn't choose peace even though they had direct access to it all along. They chose to separate themselves from God, and when we separate ourselves from God we fall into sin, and sin full blown is death (Romans 6:23). That is why we need to access peace every chance we get.

So then how are we able to guard against what surrounds us and access peace instead? By being transformed through the renewing of our minds. And how does one renew their mind? By **seeking** the prince of peace himself. Do you see the link? Jesus was called the prince of peace because no matter what opposition he faced, no matter how many enemies rose against him, even the betrayal that he faced from within, he never once repaid evil with evil. He stayed within the perfect will of the Father who is love. Even when the will of the Father didn't always feel good in the moment. Remember Jesus in his humanity said Father why has thou forsaken me? (Matthew 27:46) but, because he remained in the Father, he also said let your will be done (Luke 22:42).

You see Jesus had come to terms with his situation. Even though he had done nothing wrong, he knew that the will of the Father was going to be a

benefit far more than what his human body and mind

could comprehend or understand. Anyone else would

have been screaming, yelling, crying, and begging to get

down from the cross trying to plead their innocence.

They would have been full of rage, frustration, anxiety,

and fear because of what was directly happening to

them. But Jesus embodied peace. Throughout his three

year ministry, even unto the cross, Jesus was still

teaching us how to live in peace even while being

convicted. Now that is what I call peace that surpasses

all understanding! Jesus!!

One thing is for sure and two things are for

certain, whatever your thoughts were about peace I

pray that this description brings to you new revelation

and understanding. Peace is not for cowards. It's not for the weak. It is for the **victorious!** So by now you may be saying, well how do I apply peace as a weapon to my life when things seems so crazy right now? Well, for starters you **must saturate yourself** in the word of God. Even if this means finding all of the scriptures that relate to peace and writing them down on index cards. Place them in your room, tape them to your mirrors, stick them inside your daily planner book, tape them to the dashboard or sun roof of your car, post them on the side of your computer or on your desk at work, and say them to yourself over and over again. Continue to say them for thirty days every single day, as soon as you get up, while you are driving, when you are at work, and before going to bed, say them. Eventually they will get in your spirit and you will be able to recite them. This is called meditation.

You see, when God watches over his word to perform it, make no mistake about it he is going to bring forth the manifestation of his word because he is a God that cannot lie. **Everything** he says is **true**. This is why Jesus said **he** is the **way**, the **truth**, and the **light**. Be reminded that the truth likes to be **revealed** and on **display**, but **lies** like to live in **secret** and be **hidden**. The more you get these scriptures **down in your spirit** the more **peace** will **exude** from your spirit. So Lord God I thank you right now for my brother or my sister that is reading this book. I thank you that they have a desire for your peace, your word, and your truth. I release an activation of peace in their lives right now in the name of the Lord Jesus! I bind all hindrances, distractions, and tactics that try to keep them in a place of depression, hopelessness, unforgiveness, embarrassment or shame. Lord God reveal yourself to them and give them the peace that surpasses all understanding. I thank you for how you are going to make their sad days happy days. Thank you that your peace is upon them even right now in the name of the Lord. I declare and decree healing in their minds, in their hearts, and in their souls that shall come from the mediation of your word. I loose joy, unspeakable joy that the world will not be able to give or take away from them because they will know that it is from you. In Jesus Name!

SEEK WISE COUNSEL

When I think about the keen insight of animals I find it pretty amazing that they can usually detect disaster or trouble coming from hundreds of miles away. Their senses are so profound that at times when you see a dog suddenly jump to his feet and erect his ears upward you automatically know something is going on because the dog's posture just changed from relaxed to alert. Even though we may not be able to hear it with our natural ears, we know that God has given animals this extraordinary ability so we take heed. We begin to stand guard and suddenly we are on the lookout as well.

In past civilizations, animals were always used to help humans determine when strife was brewing. This gave humans the ability to protect themselves, come up with a plan quickly, and possibly save their families, livestock, and themselves. What I find so fascinating about God is that he does things with such intentionality and purpose that he will always warn and alert those he love. God is always going through **extreme** measures to **show us** just how much **he loves us**.

It is because of this **relentless** love that he has for us, that Satan hates us so very much. Oh yes, remember earlier in a previous chapter we talked about Job and how Satan pleaded for God to remove the covering from around him just so that he could afflict Job with pain, sickness, and loss? (Job 1:10-12) Let's **not** get it twisted because Satan is **still** trying. Often times succeeding with inflicting these same things on us today.

Satan knew that God loved Job and was well pleased with him. In the same way that Job was deeply loved, God loved us just as much too. So much, that he **gave** his **only** begotten son to **die** for the remission of **our sin** in order that we might **reign** in **eternity** with him forever. However, it doesn't stop there. God, in all of his infinite wisdom, knew that even though the shedding of Jesus's blood would justify us as righteous, that we would still be surrounded by plagues, evil, and destruction on every side. So thanks be unto God that he didn't leave us here alone.

You see Jesus said that he would never leave us as orphans, (John 14:18) so he sent us his Spirit, which is our advocate, our comforter, our help, and the one

who leads us into all truth! Yes, I am talking about the

third person of God, named Holy Spirit! The Holy Spirit

has the same knowledge, wisdom, discernment, and

understanding that Jesus does, only **we** have to be **in**

tune with **Him** in order to **comprehend** the **message** and

signal that He is giving **us**. So how do we **become** in

tune with the Holy Spirit? By taking the time to **develop**

an **intimate relationship** with him. You see Holy SPIRIT is

what gives you the spiritual ears to hear and to listen

carefully to what God is saying and wants to do in the

earth. Holy Spirit is prophetic because God is prophetic!

Therefore the more you **spend time** with God in

worship and in **prayer**, and in silence, **not** to receive

anything but just to be **saturated** in him, you will find

that your **hearing** is **heightened**. You will also recognize that your spirit is more **sensitive** to what is **happening around** you. You will also be able to discern when trouble is about to strike against you and those that you are close to.

Sometimes God will even allow us to discern when disaster is about to strike around the world. So this is why the enemy desperately wants to cut off our hearing because if God forewarns us about something that means we have the ability to do something about it. Yes I know it is a great responsibility but imagine the lives that can be changed, the solutions that can develop, simply from being obedient to what the Holy Spirit wants us to do.

Holy Spirit helps us **sharpen** our **understanding** and be piercing in our spirit so that we can **easily recognize** God's **strategy** and **follow it** through so we can win! Therefore let us be single minded in our actions and stop being ignorant about God's ways. Again, Jesus said he comes that we might have life and have it more abundantly! But we've got to exercise the power of Holy Spirit operating down on the inside of us to obtain it. We haven't even experienced half of what is available to us until we can consistently tap into and flow in what Holy Spirit is trying to do **in us** and **through us**. God says that he will pour out his wisdom liberally on anyone who asks for it (James 1:5). That means that it doesn't matter what kind of title or position someone has, God says that he will teach us his ways, and reveal to us his mysteries if we truly want it.

Don't you want to know what God has for you? Don't you want to see what he sees? Don't you want to hear how he hears? Sadly I am convinced that for a lot of us we want to be spoon fed God's word. We would much rather let the preacher, the Bible study teacher, or author take the time to study the word of God for us and then just tell us what we need to do. Yet, even when they do this, no one can develop the relationship with God for us. There are things about us that God only wants to reveal to us, no matter what we learn from someone else. It will never measure up to the things that we can learn directly from God himself. When we become dependent on someone else to feed us the truth, we stop knowing what truth sounds like outside of that particular voice and that can be detrimental. We become so weak because our hearing isn't being sharpened on a daily basis.

The enemy begins to camouflage himself through friendships, relationships, and partnerships and we have no idea that we are out of alignment and out of sync. Spiritual laziness has become so rampant that we literally are being duped into believing that we don't need the leading of the Holy Spirit until we are in times of trouble or drought. Do you know that is one of the biggest lies and tools of deception that the enemy uses against us? He knows that when we wait until danger strikes up we are actually less powerful, and more fearful because we haven't been listening or following the leading of that still small voice at any time before this point.

Let me give you an example of how counterproductive this actually is. It's just like a person who has been extremely unfit and now that they received the doctor's report decide they are going to work out. When they start, they are tired and exhausted and want to quit and give up quickly. They are not strong and their body is not used to the endurance of a vigorous workout. However for someone that has been working out consistently they can take the pressure or added stress that adding on a new vigorous routine may bring. You know, like the woman who works out regularly, gets pregnant, and still lifts weights, and works out until she's almost at her due date. Or what about those older people who we see in their seventies and eighties that can run faster than a 25 year old. That is because of their **endurance**. They have been **exercising** their muscles!

Well the same thing happens in the spirit! We must exercise our spiritual muscles by reading the word of God and deepening our relationship with Jesus and Holy Spirit through prayer. This is what strengthens us and gives us the ability to hear what Holy Spirit is saying to us and to agree with God concerning the will for our lives. The Bible says that faith comes by hearing and hearing by the word of God (Romans 10:17) so when we continue to do this daily we are actually developing ourselves, building ourselves, and birthing the confidence in ourselves to trust what the Spirit is saying. Hearing God helps us to carry out his will

successfully as according to his word. While the Spirit of

God comes to live inside of every believer that accepts

Christ as Lord and Savior, the Bible is clear that you

have to work out your own soul's salvation (Philippians

2:12). Painfully, there are many people walking around

blind to Satan's devices and on a road to utter

destruction because they do not live a life in the Spirit.

The Bible declares that:

> The person without the Spirit does not accept the
> things that come from the Spirit of God but
> considers them foolishness, and cannot
> understand them because they are discerned
> only through the Spirit. The person with the Spirit
> makes judgments about all things, but such a
> person is not subject to merely human
> judgments, for, who has known the mind of the
> Lord so as to instruct him? But we have the mind
> of Christ (1Corithians.2:14-15).

I remember when I was in prayer one morning and the Holy Spirit showed me the inside of a wet boat. I could see so clearly that the inside of the wooden boat had dry rotted due to all of the water that had seeped inside. There was also a set of feet in the boat and although I couldn't see any other part of the body I immediately knew that it was the feet of Jesus. As I began to pray fervently in the spirit, the Lord said to me that even though I would go through the storms of life and even get wet as things got rocky, he would always be with me. He said the water would never drown me out no matter how deep it became because as long as I was with him nothing would overtake me.

He began to show me Noah in the ark and how heavy the rain fell, and how strong the winds blew. Yet neither Noah nor his family were shaken! Jesus then showed me how he spoke to the storm, while he was in the boat with the disciples, to be still and it did. Through prayer the Holy Spirit was letting me know that Jesus would give me peace in the midst of every challenge and circumstance and that he would always deliver me out of my troubles if I just followed his footsteps and allowed him to lead my way.

You see the feet in the boat represented the path of Jesus, the boat represented my point of reference, and the water represented the storm. Even though I wasn't praying for myself, the fact of the matter was I had been praying for others who had been afflicted and who I knew were lost and afraid. Holy Spirit was talking back to me and revealing to me what God was saying.

When you are in tune with what the Spirit is saying,

God will confirm it with the scripture of his word and

you will know that it is Him. I thank God that I know the

voice of the Lord and that I do not need to seek or

chase a word from anyone else. I can go to the one

whose word is always true and know that he is leading

me into that truth also.

If I wasn't in tune to the leading of the Spirit I

would not have known what the Lord was trying to tell

me because I would have been too consumed with T.V.,

chatting on the phone, Facebook, YouTube, or hanging

out. I don't know about you, but I need the wise

counsel of God and his Spirit to not just be available to

me but to **overflow out of me** so that I can **withstand**

the attacks of the enemy and **not fall victim** to his

devices. Let us not forget that Satan is the father of lies and whispers quietly in our ears. If we are **not walking** in the **Spirit**, we can **mistake** the **voice** of **Satan** for our **own voice** and make decisions led by our own emotions, thoughts, and feelings instead of by the counsel and direction of the Lord.

Let us never forget that this was Adam and Eve's biggest mistake and because Satan has been studying human behavior from the beginning of time, he knows how to tickle our ears and tell us things that will move us to the point of self-destruction. So my dear sister and brother, be vigilant in your pursuit to live a life in the Spirit. Let me pray for you. Father God in the name of Jesus fill your daughter and your son right now with your Spirit. For Spirit is full of knowledge, wisdom, discernment, and understanding. Allow your Spirit to draw them like never before in the name of Jesus. Pierce their hearts and do a new thing in the very essence of their being. By the power of the Holy Ghost baptize them in the truth of your word. Intensify their ability to hear you when you are awaiting their invitation to let you in. Rule in their life, renew their mind and soul, and quicken them that they would do exactly as you said, without hindrance, hesitation, or apology. Change them Father that they may look like you, think like you, and above all else hear your voice and follow no one else's. In Jesus Name!

SPEAK TO YOUR SITUATION

You can always tell the condition of a person's heart by what comes out of their mouth. Often times we tend to think that dysfunction only operates in how we behave, but the truth of the matter is **dysfunction** is also **detected** by the **things we say**. Think about it. How many times have you actually ever done something without agreeing with it first either in your mind or out of your mouth? Never, right?! And why is that? Because it is the power of agreement with our thoughts and words that drives our decisions.

Be they good or bad, the choices that we make bear witness to what lies deep within our hearts. The Bible says that it is out of the abundance of the heart that the mouth speaks (Luke 6:45). So today I ask you the question, what are the things that are abundantly

consuming your heart? Is there anything that is hidden

within you that keeps you from unlocking the blessings

that are released through your words? Is there any

unbelief that you hold down on the inside of you? If

there is, open up your mouth and begin to release it to

your Abba Father in heaven. Don't allow it to root itself

so deep within that you cannot move in supremacy.

The word of God is clear, that we have the power to call

those things that are not as though they were (Romans

4:17) but we can only operate in that kind of authority

with **pure hearts**. Now this doesn't mean that nothing

will ever affect us because the Bible is clear that in this

world we will have tribulation (John 16:33). Yet we do

not have to become victims of it, rather we can allow

the Joy of the Lord to be our strength instead

(Nehemiah 8:10).

What you must understand is this. Having the

Lord's joy is a choice. It is a conscience decision that is

made day in and day out despite what it looks like. Am I

saying that you should never feel sadness, or loneliness,

or anger, etc.? No! Of course not. After all it was God

that gave us these emotions to be used as a tool to

communicate our needs. Let me also be clear that Jesus

who was all perfect felt all of our emotions while he

walked the earth. He knows firsthand what we go

through because he experienced life as well. The Bible

says he cried, he was sad, he even got angry when he

turned the tables over in the temple, but he continued

to walk in love! However, you can only walk in love

consistently if your heart **is not tainted** with bitterness,

envy, revenge, depression etc. Do you get the point

that I am making? So this is why the Joy of the Lord is

strength because:

> If you delight yourself in God, even when you
> don't necessarily feel like it, then he will give you
> the petitions of your heart. Commit your way to
> the Lord; trust in him also and he will do it. Cease
> from anger and abandon wrath; do not fret it
> leads only to evil. For those who do evil will be
> cut off, but those who wait for the Lord they will
> inherit the land (Psalm 37:4-9).

Isn't this reason enough to want to have the joy of the

Lord right now? Because what you have just read is a

promise that when you **choose Jesus**, instead of your

feelings, when you **trust Jesus** instead of your situation,

and when you speak those things out of your mouth to

him that you want to see happen for your life, for your family, for your future, then **He will do it**. He will make you prosperous because of your conscious decision to choose him! Jesus!!!

Just think for a moment, what God must have been thinking when he decided that he was going to create the world and fill it with light, color, laughter, people, animals, and all kinds of beauty in the sky and the sea. I mean can you imagine what it would be like to sit in a dark room that is pitch black with nothing in it but you? What words would you utter out of your mouth? Would it be words of fear? Apprehension? Doubt? Or could you speak life, and hope? Essentially that is exactly what God did when he created the universe. Although it was dark to the natural eye, he spoke what he wanted that darkness to be and BOOM, just like that it **became** light. Without a second thought, he **declared life** in the **midst of darkness** and produced **living creatures**!

I mean when we really stop to inhale the air, and look up at the beautiful blue sky, and see the bright shining sun, or the glimmering moon, it's hard to believe that all of this was just a void. That at one time, none of this existed but if you allow God to have his way in your heart then these spiritual principles will become your reality. When you are operating from a pureness of heart, God will allow you to speak in dark places and bring forth his light! He will allow you to experience a dry season and declare the rain. He will put you in a hopeless situation and give you the ability to decree healing and guess what? He will show up every time! Because God's glory reigns supreme! What's so incredible is that he wants that glory to work through us and in us by the power that he shares with us.

Nothing has changed from when he first created Adam and Eve. The Bible says that they had dominion over the fish in the sea and the birds in the sky and over every living creature that moved on the ground (Genesis 1:28). Adam and Eve had **authority that came from God** and as long as they were **choosing** him they were able to see what they desired come to pass. They could speak to their situation and see it manifest right before their very eyes. It wasn't until they allowed unbelief to consume their hearts that they gave their authority and power away and so too it is with us! That through Jesus Christ we have been given dominion to speak to the mountain and it will be taken up and thrown into the sea (Matthew 21:21). Unfortunately, we can **choose** to **allow** the enemy to **reign OVER** us, causing the posture of our hearts to bear fruit of disobedience, dysfunction, and defeat that is reflected through our thoughts, words, and deeds.

Today I want you to **choose life**. Declare that you are triumphant. Advocate for your future. Demand and stake your claim. Let me tell you what I love about God the most. It's that he is the Lion of Judah. He has a tenacious roar that causes his word to sharpen, and strengthen. To build and break. To purge and purify. Because He is **fire** and **water**. So when you **come into** agreement with what the **Lord says** and **you begin to speak those things through prayer,** and **through reading the word a loud,** then your faith **will ignite a flame inside of you that no enemy can destroy.** The **Holy Ghost fire within you** will **burn all of those hidden things that has kept you bound** and **reveal to you the true plan of God** on which you will be able to stand.

So Father God in the name of Jesus, I thank you for your child, your son, your daughter, whomever is reading this right now. I release and speak over their life words of blessings, words of faith, words of wisdom, words of joy, words of peace, words of comfort, words of strength, words of authority, words of power, and words of love. Now God by the power of your son Jesus the Christ, raise them up and fill their belly with rivers of living water so that every dirty area in their life becomes clean. Saturate them with the power of your Spirit that what comes out of their mouth is boldness, confidence, and the assurance that can only come through you.

I declare a heart transplant in their life now Father in the name of Jesus! Speak to them through your word, empower them through your Spirit, ignite them in prayer, and reveal your glory throughout their life! I pull down every stronghold of bitterness, rejection, isolation, depression, pride, failure, fear, insecurity, scrutiny, idolatry, hate, false identity and send it back to the pit of hell from which it comes. Father God wash them with your word which is abundant life, fullness, and unspeakable joy! I release it now Father and I declare it finished! In the name of the

Lord Jesus!

ARMOR YOURSELF WITH THE SHIELD OF FAITH

I decided to save this chapter for last because I believe that it is the one that ties all of the others together, solidifying who you are, and ultimately where you are going. Before fully surrendering my life to Christ I was a victim on a ferocious rollercoaster that paralyzed and taunted me. While I knew there was more to life than what I was living I couldn't seem to obtain it. I had always had tangible things but even with that I wasn't operating at maximum potential. There was something within me that yearned to birth but I didn't have the right formula to produce it.

It's like the beginning of a pregnant woman's experience. To the naked eye, she cannot physically see that there is a seed that is growing in her body, but she feels and knows that it is there. I was tired of aborting what I felt was inside of me. I was tired of running back to familiar places, faces, and things. I wanted a **new thing to happen** not just **for me**, not just **in me** but **through me**. I was tired of developing things with what I already had. I wanted to **pull out of me** what I felt way **down on the inside** but knew I **didn't have the ability to do on my own**. I mean let's face it, if I had the ability to do it, it would have already been done! I wanted what I could not see but what I knew was there.

What I wanted was **purpose.** What I **needed was active faith**. For the Bible says that **now** faith is the substance of things hoped for and the evidence of things not seen (Hebrews 11:1). You see it is the **now** faith that moves mountains. It is the **now** faith that open doors. It is the **now** faith that makes impossibility seem easy. Do you know how to operate in **now** faith? Because the one thing that is crystal clear is that if it is now faith that moves, then it is inactive faith that stagnates.

One of the things that I have always heard about faith is that its opposite is fear. While this is true I challenge you to think about whether it was fear that caused Adam and Eve to eat that fruit. You see we often think of fear as trembling and shaking but fear can also include trying to manipulate and have control over our own future. Fear is **operating outside** of the **will of God**. For the Bible says that God has not given us a spirit of fear but of power, love, and a sound mind (2

Timothy 1:7). Therefore, fear is a ferocious rollercoaster that comes from Satan. On this rollercoaster you have doubts, go back and forth in your mind, move forward and backward, don't know whether you are coming or going.

Did you know that is exactly what Adam and Eve were doing? They were operating in the fear that God was keeping something from them that would be beneficial for them. They were trying to control their own destinies and it was because of that fear that led them into their disobedience. Since that is the case, we know that sin is a byproduct of fear and if sin is a result of fear then it is obvious that **fear can heavily determine** whether or not the **purposes for our lives come into fruition**. This can happen if we **do not carry out the**

instructions that God has given us. You see what we must really come to understand is that **sin is designed to abort the plan of God**. Its mission is **to take out as many destinies as possible** so that change doesn't happen, freedom can't happen, justice can't happen, or at the very least, to as little and tiny as possible. Ultimately, as long as we give in to sin then we do not have to address or accept the plan of God for our lives but who wants to live like that when **God purposed us to be prosperous!**

What you must understand is the minute you **decide** you are going to **walk with** God that is when **you need** to have the **grace** of God. Because without it you cannot successfully triumph over your fears! Remember, fear is designed to keep you immobile and unfruitful. The more we operate in fear the more we give in to sin. You see sin's desire is to rule over us and make us forget that God is ruler over it, but it is the grace of God that will give us the ability to stand and face fear head on! Do you know why? Because the Bible says where sin abounds grace abounds all the more (Romans 5:20).

This means that even though there will be a struggle to think your own thoughts, go your way, do your own thing, talk yourself out of thinking that you are qualified, or capable, the grace of God will give you the ability to move forward. Now that sounds like an incredible God who supplies miraculous mercies and that is because at the end of the day God's grace to us is an extension of his love! His love **has always been** and still is a **gift** to us. He created us **because** he **loves us**, and even when humanity fell from grace, he had a plan that restored us back to it. What we must realize is that grace doesn't come without faith, rather it is a by-product of it.

For the Bible says that we are saved by grace through faith, so even though Jesus saved us by dying on the cross for our sins, we must **accept** and **believe** that he did this in order to receive it. Once we receive this grace, it will empower and strengthen our faith. Faith causes you to be steadfast. Faith causes you to be unmovable. Faith causes you to defy odds. Faith causes you to crack glass ceilings. Faith causes you to triumph over your enemies. Faith causes you to stand up against opposition and win and it is your faith that will give you the grace to walk victoriously! Hallelujah!

One of my favorite stories in the Bible is about David and Goliath. Here was this little boy who wasn't any bigger that an average sized teenager or so I could imagine, that faced a Philistine giant toe to toe and killed him. With a sling shot and one hit he defeated this giant. When it was time for David to go and face Goliath he didn't come up with an excuse about why he couldn't do it or say let's wait until tomorrow. He simply said "LORD, who delivered me from the paw of the lion and from the paw of the bear, He will deliver me from the hand of this Philistine" (1 Samuel 17:37). It wasn't by David's strength or power but it was by his incredible faith!

If having on the armor of faith could do that for David just imagine what it can do for us! You see, David was not focused on **what** was happening, he was focused on **how** it was going to happen and that was by standing on the rock of his salvation which was the everlasting Lord! What we have to realize is that David's **faith** gave him the **grace** to fight **from** a place of **victory** because his **faith** had **empowered** him to do so! We can have all the armor in the world in our possession but if we don't use it then what good can it do us? Your ability to put on your armor of faith **is your strategy!** Yes, I think I need to say that again. **It is your strategy!!** When the Bible says that faith without works is dead (James 2:26) this is exactly what it is talking about.

Let me give you an example. Think about all the clothes you have in your closet and how every day you have the ability to put on something new or at least something different. Now think a little harder. Has there ever been a time when you accidentally ran across a shirt that you haven't worn in a while and then you put it on and it goes perfect with that pair of pants? You know that pair you have been saving all of this time because you thought you didn't have the right combination to go with it? So what just happened? Well let me tell you. You took an old shirt that was sitting hidden in a drawer or hanging in a closet and you gave it a function. The shirt just went from irrelevant to purposeful. However, prior to that you had never even considered the value of the shirt. Either you overlooked it, pushed it in the corner, or simply grew tired of it because you had it for so long.

Well that is exactly how the armor of faith works. It is right there in your possession, waiting to be used. Often times taken for granted and right there at our finger tips. Waiting to be given purpose, waiting to demonstrate its value, and waiting to be put with the right situation so that it can be executed. However, **you've got to put it on!** You've got to realize that it is in fact the **attire** that you need in order to **render yourself effective** in whatever you are trying to **accomplish, overcome, defeat or endure.**

When the enemy says that you can't have it, you can't do it, you can't birth it, you can't lead it, or you aren't worth it, it is the armor of faith that will destroy these yokes. It is the armor of faith that will destroy

every lie and it is the armor of faith that will remind you

that you can and you will! So Father God in the name of

Jesus I thank you for the activation of faith that only

comes from you. I loose it now over your daughter,

over your son, over the one that may be lost but is now

finding their way back home. Father God you said in

your word that it is not your will that even one shall

perish (2 Peter 3:9)! So I thank you that you are drawing

your children unto you right now because there is more

that you want to show them. There is greater works

that you want them to demonstrate. Higher levels that

you want them to achieve. So I loose **now** faith into

their lives and I loose a revelation into a **deeper**

understanding of what that means. **I break the bondage**

of sin and I bind the spirit of fear. Lord God I declare

your clarity, your power, your strength, your guidance,

your love into the depths of their very soul and spirit

now that it will take root and grow and bear good fruit in

Jesus Name!

NOTE FROM THE AUTHOR:

To my readers,

Thank you so much for taking the time to purchase this book. I may not know where you are on your journey but my heart's desire is that you can take something from this book, apply it to your life, and receive incredible results. Know that there is nothing too hard for God if you only trust him. It is not enough to know about him. You must take the time to get to know him and believe who he is.

I want you to know that if someone would have told me 12 years ago that today I would have written this book, one that is filled with the understanding and knowledge of God I would have thought that they were **insane**. My life was **nothing** like it is **today. I wasn't saved** and **I laughed** at people **who believed in the power of Jesus.** But, today **I know** that **He is the Resurrected King.**

He is the **only one that saved me from a life** that was **spiraling out of control.** If I didn't **find Jesus, I know** that I **was going to die.** My **self-destructive behaviors** and **need for wholeness** made me an **open target for the enemy.** He had a **hit out on my life** but **God saved me in the nick of time.** His plan was **greater** than any one that I had ever **imagined or dreamed** about. I am so glad that when he called my name, I said **yes. It wasn't an easy** road but **it was worth it.** What I didn't know then that I absolutely know now, is that **without the Light of Christ** we **can only see** things based on our **own perception.** It is in that perception that we give Satan the power to manipulate us, con us, and keep us from fulfilling our true destinies.

Was I successful by the world's definition? **Yes**. But there is **no way** that I could have **unlocked the hidden potential within me without being released from** the **bondage** that **sin had over me.** Make no mistake about it, **your talents**, no matter how great, **don't compare** to **your accomplishments** that **can only come from your true identity that is in Christ Jesus.** If you don't know him as your Lord and Savior **you can accept him right now in this moment**. No one has to be with you, for God sees everything and he is right there with you. **Repeat these words out loud so that he can immediately enter your heart.** I admit that I am a **sinner today**. Because of my sin I deserve death, but I don't **have to die** because I **believe that Jesus Christ paid the price of death for me on the cross. Holy Spirit come live on the inside of me.** Teach me, help me, lead me and guide me into all truth. **Today I receive my salvation! I am saved, I am accepted, and I am set free.**

I pray that this book **blesses** you and gives you a **strategy** for how to **become victorious, walk victorious,** and **remain victorious** for all the days of your life.

Peace and Blessings,

Safuja Terrell

ABOUT THE AUTHOR

Safiya Terrell is a woman who is sold out for God. Safiya is a young prophetic voice who has a heart for evangelism and believes it is her God given assignment to preach the Gospel to the young and the old, across all cultures. She believes in the power of God's supernatural healing whether it be through prayer, words, or laying on of hands. She is currently in training to become a licensed minister and she is also a prophetic intercessor. For several years she has taught and mentored the young generation on how to live a life for Christ successfully.

Safiya gets most of her revelation from her alone time with God and she is growing in her prophetic gifting. Through hearing God's voice and following his leading Safiya has experienced encounters with God that has forever changed her life. More than everything else, Safiya believes that knowing God only comes through a deep and intimate relationship with him. Her time spent in God's presence is where she says "all transformation takes place. Separate from that you are just following rules, rituals, and religion."

You are Victorious is a book that was birthed out of a spiritual battle that Safiya had to face and endure during one of the most challenging yet rewarding seasons of her life. Before birthing this book the Lord had already prepared Safiya that she was about to go into battle that would shake her to the very core. In the weeks leading up to writing this book the Lord began to speak to Safiya in her quiet time and began to show her what to do when the storm came. As she prayed fervently to the Lord he began to give her strategic insight on exactly how to endure, maintain peace, and win! Today she realizes that it was the process necessary to produce in her a greater faith, a greater walk, greater insight, and also a greater ability to write while in the Spirit! Her trust in the Lord is greater now than ever before and she has learned that with God on your side **YOU TRULY ARE VICTORIOUS!**

MEET THE AUTHOR

Safiya Amira Terrell believes it is her mandate from God to reach others by teaching them through her writing and preaching how to walk in the will of God. For this is the definition of true success!

TO REACH SAFIYA AMIRA TERRELL

facebook	Safiya Amira Terrell
Instagram	Safiya_Amira_Terrell
📍 Periscope	Safiya Amira Terrell
▶ YouTube	Safiya Amira Terrell